FALLING OUT OF LOVE WITH IVAN SOUTHALL

Gabrielle Carey published her first co-written book, *Puberty Blues,* while still in her teens. She has since written biography, autobiography, memoir, essays and articles. Her book *Moving Among Strangers* (UQP, 2013), about the Australian poet and novelist Randolph Stow, was the joint winner of the 2014 Prime Minister's Award for Non-Fiction and short-listed for the 2015 National Biography Award.

Since learning to read, Gabrielle has regularly fallen in and out of love with her favourite authors. Her first love was Ivan Southall, her next was James Joyce and her current affair is with Elizabeth von Arnim.

FALLING OUT OF LOVE WITH IVAN SOUTHALL

GABRIELLE CAREY

Australian Scholarly

First published 2018 by
Australian Scholarly Publishing Pty Ltd
7 Lt Lothian St Nth, North Melbourne, Vic 3051
Tel: 03 9329 6963 / Fax: 03 9329 5452
enquiry@scholarly.info / www.scholarly.info

ISBN 978-1-925801-53-8

Cover: Ivan Southall by Andrew Southall.
Drawing 2018. Private Collection
Cover design: Wayne Saunders

Acknowledgments

The writing and research of this book was supported by the Australia Council for the Arts, a National Library of Australia Fellowship, a UTS Research Equity Fellowship and a Varuna Eric Dark Flagship Fellowship.

The final editing of the book was greatly assisted by Maisie Fieschi.

I want to thank the staff of the National Library of Australia, in particular Ralph Sanderson and Andrew Sergeant. I am also indebted to the Southall family – Joy Southall, Elizabeth Barber and Susan Southall. And I would like to extend a special thank you to my sincere friend, Drew Southall.

What I took to be indigestion turned out to be a tad more serious, a manifestation of a love soon to cease, of a love that never really got off the drawing board. My father and I never hit it off. At best, he failed to hide his frustration with his son, though in later years did pay certain bills I couldn't, or wouldn't; in later years tolerated his wife, my mother, but mainly died oblivious of his lifelong courage, in particular, his achievement, and thinking hardly anything at all about words, about the opinions of others, about fuchsias.

Andrew Southall

The last time I was in Canberra, I had a near-death experience.

Twenty-one years ago, I came to the national capital to take up my first teaching post. I had applied to coordinate a course called "Professional Writing", even though I didn't believe in the concept of writers as professionals and certainly didn't know any. During the interview for the job, I had sat opposite the panel, attempting to demonstrate professionalism at the same time as distracting attention from my maternity smock, hoping they would assume I was plump rather than pregnant. Being polite, they didn't ask, and being cagey, I didn't tell them.

The baby was expected to arrive no later than 25 October, the last day for handing in my final marks for the students. But October came and went. And then the first week of November, the second, and the third. I tried inhaling clary sage, horse-riding, having sex in unconventional positions, all to no avail. The doctor was beginning to talk about inducement, which would have meant going to hospital, something I was determined not to do. Having grown up in a family that rejected all mainstream practices, such as giving birth in a maternity ward, I refused to acknowledge male, obstetric expertise, even if it meant risking my life.

The midwife suggested going to the cinema to take my mind off trying to go into labour. Perhaps if I could stop thinking about it, it might happen. As I was in suburban Canberra with nothing else to do, I took her advice. The film was *Angel Baby,* about two schizophrenics who fall in love and have a baby. I was thrilled to see that not all cinema had gone the way of Hollywood and that these two marginalized lovers might have a happy ending. So it came as a shock, in the final scenes, when the young mother died while in labour. I came out of the cinema scowling. "As *if* people in the first world die in childbirth anymore! How ridiculous!"

Finally, on 17 November, I felt a sudden sharp pain in my thighs. He was on his way. Except at that point I didn't know it was a "he"; I had refused the offer of prior knowledge, just as I had refused all of the other antenatal tests and advice for "older mothers" – I was 37 – including the warning that having a baby at home, at my age, was dangerous and irresponsible.

Early the next morning, at the end of a very long night accompanied by a midwife and my then partner, I lay in the bath with a baby in my arms. I looked at his genitals and thought: "So that's why you're such a little troublemaker!"

I was so happy that I didn't realise I was losing blood at a near-fatal rate. Not until I was in the ambulance with a uniformed paramedic strapping black harnesses to my limbs, like large blood pressure belts, did I understand that my life was in the balance.

"This is just so we can pump blood from your extremities to your vital organs," the paramedic explained calmly.

The following morning, my mother came to visit me in a clean, private room of Woden Hospital as I was receiving my second blood infusion. She was so shocked by my ghostly pale appearance that she went away quietly to prepare a funeral.

I later learned that the post-partum haemorrhage, which couldn't be staunched until I'd seen a doctor, had indeed been life-threatening. I had lost approximately two-thirds of my blood. Thanks to generous blood donations from strangers, I survived, although I never regained my former vigour. In exchange for bringing my son into the world, I lost some elemental energy. Nevertheless, I've always felt a debt to Canberra. If I'd been in Sydney, the ambulance may not have been so quick and efficient, nor the trip to the hospital so rapid. If there had been a delay of half an hour, I may well have ended up like Jacqueline McKenzie in *Angel Baby.*

* * *

More than twenty years after the birth of my son, Canberra is again the backdrop for a personal drama. I have arrived on a mission to track down a letter at the National Library amid a dangerous crisis of faith that keeps me awake at night and causes regular panic attacks by day. My psychiatrist has prescribed the maximum dose of mirtazapine, a toxic medication that barely takes the edge off my intense anxiety. But the problem, which feels like another haemorrhage but of a deeper, more complex kind, is not something that can be fixed by prescription pharmaceuticals.

All my life I have put my faith in books and literature and writing. It is how I have created meaning and purpose. But of late, I have begun to wonder whether novels and poetry, with their webs of literary illusions, have actually conspired to ruin me; whether what I believed to be sources of wisdom are actually pernicious forces that constantly lead me astray.

My psychic dependence on books only became clear when I had a dream about being swept up in a cyclone and the only solid thing I could find to hold onto was a bookshelf. Needless to say, it wasn't weighty enough to keep my feet on the ground.

It feels as if all those years, and all those books, both written and read, have been leading to this moment; a moment where I sit in judgment of myself and my vocation. Something like a Carmelite nun, who, after fifty years, looks down at her worn hands and her worn habit, and suddenly and irrevocably loses faith.

In order to understand how I got here, I need to go back to the beginning, to the books that formed me. From my earliest awakenings as a reader there were three books that had struck me deeply, perhaps too deeply: *The Little Prince* by Antoine de Saint-Exupéry, *The Coral Island* by J.M. Ballantyne and Ivan Southall's *To the Wild Sky.* Each one, I realise now, is about a child or children abandoned in a foreign, wild and dangerous place, uninhabited by adults. Each one, in a sense, is a story of shipwreck. What, I wonder, was the root of their deep appeal?

Was I simply hungry for adventure? Or did I unconsciously seek heroic suffering? Something that would test me to the edge of endurance? I suspect now that the qualities I admired most in an adult were courage and bravery and I wanted desperately to develop and prove those characteristics in myself. I look back on my life and see that at every turn, I chose the path of most resistance, deliberately seeking out hardship for reasons that seemed inexplicable to my family, and often to myself. One decision after another led to a new, intensified level of endurance, like a game with increasing levels of difficulty or the classic fairy tale whose protagonist is handed challenges of greater and greater risk, all in the quest to get the ring or find the chalice or uncover the key or whatever symbol is standing in for self-realisation.

I distinctly remember the moment I turned the last page of *To the Wild Sky* because it was when I made the very first of those fateful, deliberately difficult decisions: I decided to become a writer.

To the Wild Sky, published in 1967, when I was eight, was the book that started it all. It is a story of children travelling in a light plane when the pilot has a heart attack and dies, leaving his young passengers utterly alone, mid-air.

Which is pretty much exactly how I feel now.

* * *

Although mostly unread and unknown to young people of the present generation, in the 1960s and 1970s, Ivan Southall was a literary superstar. Selling in the hundreds of thousands and translated into over twenty languages, Southall produced twenty-three books for children and was the only Australian to be awarded the Carnegie Medal. While Southall was reviled by some critics, and accused of racism, sadism, and even raping the child mind, his young readers loved him. Many wrote to him to say so. I want to find out if I was one of them.

So I begin my adventures into the Ivan Southall archives at the National Library with self-interest. I have always been a compulsive letter-writer, so it was just conceivable that I, like so many other children, had felt compelled to put pen to paper while in the after-glow of reading *To the Wild Sky*. If I could find such a letter, I might be able to recall what that original urge to write felt like.

After two days of reading through twenty-five folders of Southall's correspondence, I realise two of the folders from 1968, the period in which I would have written, are missing. And in any case, by this stage, I am so ensconced in the hundreds of letters from other nine-, ten- and eleven-year-olds that my initial intention falls away and I find myself on a different quest altogether. I am not sure exactly what; I just know that I am enthralled with these children from the 1960s and 1970s. I love their handwriting, their candidness, their stories about their pets, their complaints about siblings, their ambitions, their reports of daily mundanities, and I especially love their spelling mistakes. "I past all my exams," writes Janie proudly, "and on Sunday I got 15 Easter eggs." "I don't think wrighting books is for me," confesses Linda. "I am going to become a nurse if I can. I am a guide and I am going for my First Aid badge." Three cheers for Linda! What a sensible decision. My mother and grandmother were both nurses. Why hadn't I followed in their footsteps?

It's true that over the years of writing books I too have received a number of fan letters but nothing as charming and certainly not in these numbers. I am ashamed to confess that, for reasons I do not understand, I often found myself incapable of responding. Perhaps I detected a sense of neediness or an attempt to break through the boundary between writer and reader, a boundary I treasure. In comparison, Southall's openness in his diligent, neatly dated responses is admirable.

These days, of course, a hand-written letter to an author would be a rarity. She or he might receive an email or perhaps a response to a blog but the era of rustic intimacy implied by the hand-written letter – its enforced waiting for a response and its necessary imposition of patience, is over.

Although many of the letters recount everyday events from the ordinary, comparatively sheltered lives of children from that era, most begin with adulation for the author and attest to a wide and devoted audience:

Dear Mr Southall,

I'm writing to you because I just read To the Wild Sky. It was a beaut book and I loved reading it. In the story, they landed at Molineaux Island. Was this island fictional? I've looked in about four atlases and can't find it.

Susan, Glen Iris

Dear Mr Southall,

I have just read your book Ash Road and I have found it very exciting. I am very impressed by the way you describe the young people. What I'm trying to say is that you would have to know young people to have written about them and I think you know young people very, very well.

Sincerely yours,
Mary, Ohio

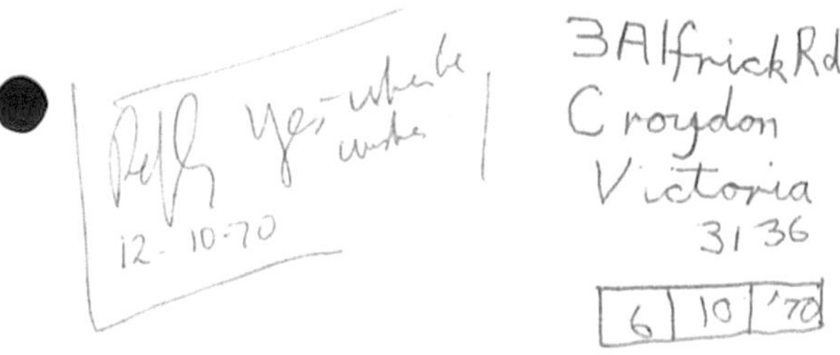

12-10-70

3 Alfrick Rd.
Croydon
Victoria
3136

6 | 10 | '70

Dear Mr. Southall,

I wonder if I could come and see you some time.

I know that you are probably tied up writing one of ~~those~~ sensational books of yours but I just want ~~to~~ say, that seeing you are a marvellous author, maybe I could ask you a few questions and may be you could tell me a few things. PTO

I would be very pleased to meet you as I have a few things to show you.

Yours sincerely
Peter Dean

RSPV

At the top of each letter in Southall's handwriting is the word "Reply" and a date. No correspondent, as far as I can tell, fails to receive a response. Peter (above) gets a personal invitation to visit the author in person. At the top of his letter, Southall writes: "Reply, Yes, when he wishes. 12-10-70".

Predictably, one of the most common questions in letters from young readers is about how to become a writer. Southall responds with great earnestness to each enquiry:

Dear Mr Southall,

I'm writing a story called "The Visitors from Outer Space". It will be a good story if I can find it and finish it. It's lost around the house somewhere. How do you keep your mind on your work? Once I start working on something I hardly ever finish it.

Yours truly,

Peter

Dear Peter,

What you must do is use a notebook or an exercise book for your stories and put a bright red cover on it. The only way to finish anything, Peter, is to keep on going until you get to the finish. There is simply no other way.

Sincerely,
Ivan Southall

I admire Southall's directness. I have been teaching creative writing for twenty years now but have never dared offer this most obvious advice: "The only way to finish anything is to keep on going until you get to the finish." It's not what creative writing students pay for. They don't want to hear that "there is simply no other way." They are hoping you will let them in on a secret. Indeed, they have paid *good money* for that secret, which is why so many of them feel disappointed when they realise that there is no secret except keeping going.

Southall replies at length to twelve-year-old Diane, who hopes to develop a career as a writer:

Dear Diane,

Thank you very much for your letter. You have asked a very difficult question – "how does one go about becoming a successful author?" – and I will do my best with it, but I know it will not be a complete answer because I don't really think it can be answered completely, certainly not by me anyway.

First of all, what is a successful author? Are we to judge him by the money he makes or by the quality of the books he writes? You mentioned my "Simon Black" books. By average standards they have been successful but, goodness me, one could never call them good books, they cannot be called literature, because they are not and do not pretend to be. I started writing when I was very young because I felt I knew what young people wanted to read about and as I have grown older I think each one has been a little better than the one before …

I tend to believe that the person who wants to be a writer will be a writer if he has determination and perseverance. I do think that writers are born, not made … It's not easy. Unless you have another job or a private income you will probably be very poor for many years … Most of the "successful" writers just manage to scrape along, some years earning thousands, other years earning almost nothing. Speaking for myself, reasonably successful by Australian standards, I own my own home because I built it myself little by little, I run a car but it's an old one, I cannot afford to send my children to colleges, but I'm happy. I'm doing what I want to do.

I don't want to discourage you, but it would not be right of me to paint a glowing picture and leave out the shadows. It's very hard work.

My very best wishes to you and to all the members of your class and I wish you luck, fulfilment and happiness in whatever you attempt to do in life.

Your sincere friend,
Ivan Southall

"Your sincere friend" is such a touching and tender way to sign off. I don't think I have ever considered my readers as sincere friends. Possibly this is why I have a readership of three and Southall had hundreds of thousands.

If I had received such a letter, would the warning of poverty have discouraged me from trying to be a writer? Not at all. I would have thought it was romantic. I would have considered it an opportunity to demonstrate my devotion and courage. Once you've fallen in love with the idea of being a writer, it's just like any other kind of falling in love: no rational argument will dissuade you.

In searching through the correspondence, I find I am not the only child whose experience of reading Southall made them want to be an author themselves:

Dear Mr Southall,

I'm writing to say that I love reading your books. I am reading Ash Road and Over the Top. I wish to grow up to be an author and write wonderful stories like you. When I read your books, I feel I'm really there.

Bye for now Mr Southall,

Julie

I remember clearly the moment I got to the end of *To the Wild Sky* and felt an uncontainable excitement, like someone who had just fallen in love. And it was in the grip of this momentary infatuation that I made my hasty decision to be a writer.

Now here I am, fifty years later, attempting to re-discover the impetus for that fateful decision, a decision that has left me deeply doubtful, a decision that is *all Southall's fault.*

* * *

Before *To the Wild Sky,* Southall began his long career in writing for children with a series of nine Biggles-style adventure books published over a period of eleven years by Australian publisher Angus & Robertson. The books are based on a superhero pilot named Simon Black, with titles such as *Simon Black in Peril* (1951), *Simon Black in Space* (1952), and *Simon Black in China* (1954). Books about boys, for boys, which Southall would later dismiss as not deserving of the description "literature". "Simon Black was six-feet tall, black-haired, skinny, incredibly clever, incredibly handsome – me, you see, my superego," Southall told Hazel de Berg. "Typical of the time but mimicking in a way the books for boys I'd read as a child. All I was doing was perpetuating the old British imperial myth."

On the back cover of my 1958 edition of *Simon Black and the Space Men* is a photo of the young and remarkably handsome Southall in his Royal Australian Air Force (RAAF) uniform. Was that perhaps the beginning of my infatuation? His looks, like his books, are enigmatic.

Southall's departure from fanciful adventure stories for boys happened suddenly, one rainy afternoon in 1959. He tells this story repeatedly in letters, in conversations, and in interviews. As he explains in a letter to a reader in 1971:

In 1959 in the living room of my home, then at Monbulk, Victoria, I asked my brother a question: "What would happen to our children if they were left on their own and we were not here to look after them?" He thought they would die, probably in a short time. I thought about it for a year and then decided to find out in a story. So I took some of those children who had been with us that day, and a few that I knew, changed their names, put them in an imaginary town called Hills End and then discovered the story you read in the book. I didn't know how it was going to work out and I didn't know whether the children would live or die. To me it was a real adventure.

Hills End (1962) is the first of Southall's trilogy of "survival stories" in which young protagonists are faced with disasters. This first follows the fates of seven children trapped in a cave while storms and floods wreak destruction on their town; the second, *Ash Road* (1965), chronicles a bushfire; and the third, *To the Wild Sky,* a plane crash.

Southall later describes *Hills End* as "an abrupt and major change of course that came to be regarded, worldwide, as a new departure in literature for children." A final draft was delivered to his long-time publisher Angus & Robertson in 1959, but there were serious reservations about the author's dramatic change in tone and subject matter from the Simon Black books. One of the readers for the publisher thought that it was too mature for young children and that "the psychological exploration of motives and moods, (although interesting) [were] a little out of tune for the juvenile". The question of whether his stories were or were not suitable for children would dog Southall for the rest of his professional life. Angus & Robertson editor Beatrice Davis disagreed with the reader, realising that the manuscript was the best that Southall had ever produced. The book was released in Sydney and London by A&R in 1962 and in the USA by St Martin's Press in 1963.

What happened next was something that neither the author nor the publisher could have imagined. In 1963, *Hills End* was included in the list of the *New York Times*' "Books of the Year" and chosen by the American Library Association as one of fifty-five titles recognised as "Notable Children's Books" of that year. *Hills End* would go on to be translated into ten languages, and developed twice into a television mini-series, firstly in France, and then in Australia. In Sweden, *Hills End* was dramatised for radio, and in Japan produced as a musical stage show. Sales eventually ran into the hundreds of thousands.

Southall had clearly struck a chord and his young readers write to express their appreciation:

Dear Mr Southall,

I just have finished reading Hills End. I have read hundreds of books but never have I read one twice. Hills End I have read thrice. It's the best book in my library and the best I've read in all my life (12 years, 13 yrs come May).

Your faithful reader,
Robert

P.S. I am telling everyone about Hills End.

Dear Mr Southall,

We have enjoyed your story Hills End and have had pleasure in reading it. Our class have designed a map of Hills End, of what we imagined it to be like. We have had difficulty in placing the township road to Stanley and the river Magnus, and would like you to correct the mistakes we have probably made.

Yours sincerely,
Jillian on behalf of Grade Six,
St Mary's College, Hobart

Buninyong primary school
no 1290
simpson st Buninyong
Vic 3357
7-6-76

Dear Mr Southhall

I have read five of your books and I like them all Hills end is my favorite.

I live in a small goldmining town in western Victoria my great great grandfather was king of the spliters when Buninyong just began. We have an extinct volcano and the town is at the foot of it.

I am ten years old and could I please have your autograph.

Yours sincerely
Tim Simpson

Rep'd 4-9-76

What is it about *Hills End* that makes it so exceptional? It is certainly dramatic. The little town is left in ruins and the children are alone without shelter or food or an adult to protect them. But there is something else that is new, which isn't just about drama. Southall would later comment that *Hills End* is his favourite because "it was the first book I ever wrote that had something useful to say." The "useful thing" it has to say is that even amid disaster, children are capable of rising to the occasion. In *Hills End*, Southall lets children know that, whatever the circumstances, he has *faith* in them. And it is a message that children, including my nine-year-old self, were thrilled to hear. Reading Southall made me feel I had someone on my side. Despite the book brimming over with danger, the effect was to make me feel safe.

In the introduction to a 2013 re-issue of *Hill's End* by Text Publishing, author James Maloney writes:

> Southall's ground-breaking theme in this novel is presented early and in the starkest possible manner: that adults believe children cannot survive on their own, that without the experience, good sense and courage of grown-ups they must inevitably fall into helplessness and chaos. The concluding chapter of *Hills End* is a private nod between the young protagonists and the children

> who read it … Don't wait for grown-ups to give you credit for your fortitude, he is saying, because ultimately you only have to prove it to yourself to be certain such qualities lie within you. Southall paved the way for John Marsden's novels twenty-five years later. Marsden's *Tomorrow When the War Began* series is in many ways a grand expansion of Southall's scenario in *Hills End.*

John Marsden himself admits to being impressed by Southall as a young reader:

> He did have a level of psychological awareness that I probably wasn't aware of as a reader but it was very effective. I think he was aware of the unconscious or at least endowed his characters with unconscious minds more than previous generations had done.

In other words, Southall's dramatic material is as much internal as external. As Southall says: "I am trying to introduce children to the idea that their greatest adventures, their greatest moments, will belong to what goes on inside."

This is certainly an idea that I internalised as a child. The interior life has always been more real to me than the exterior. But I've recently concluded that the perpetual introspection of a writer's life is not a healthy or happy way of living. I'm now wondering if I should have taken my high school careers advisor's recommendation and become a florist instead.

* * *

I begin to wonder about the man himself, particularly his sense of vocation and absolute insistence on making his living as a writer, despite the overwhelming difficulties. Southall was that very rare of writers, a genuine professional, scraping by from one royalty cheque to the next. But his success had not come easily. His father, who had always been physically weak, died after a period of deterioration in hospital, leaving Ivan, as his eldest son, obliged to leave school. "At fourteen and five months, I started working like a man at several jobs simultaneously," writes Southall. The man who was to spend his life writing for and about children had in fact been robbed of a significant part of his own childhood. This may explain, in part, why so many of Southall's boy characters are suddenly and brutally thrown into roles that demand adult responsibility. It may also explain why many of his books struggle with ideas of masculinity and the way in which boys make the treacherous journey from boyhood to manhood.

Like his father, Ivan was not masculine, in a physical sense. Nowadays he might have found a way to fit in by joining the legion of slim hipsters but in the 1940s and 1950s he felt inadequate. "I am not over-blessed with manly strength," he writes. "I'm conscious of a thin body. I dislike standing in a public shower, or sunbaking on a beach. I feel eyes on me, my body worries me." Despite attempts at body-building and weight-lifting, Southall couldn't live up to the ideal of the Australian male and it was a deficiency he felt all his life.

Even at fourteen, Southall knew he wanted to write. He had his first story published when he was twelve in the Melbourne *Herald Junior,* and sent off a new story every week to the same publication for the next three years. But his mother wasn't impressed with her son's aspirations. "He should be told that writers starve," she commented.

At fifteen, Southall started as a copyboy with the Melbourne *Herald* in their Flinders Street office, running messages and making tea for the sub-editors. In 1937 the editor of *Weekend Magazine* published Ivan's first non-fiction article, "Chicken Sexers are Busy".

> He sits with a 12-hour-old chicken grasped between his fingers. He gives it a quick glance under a 300 candle power globe, and places it in

> a box among dozens of others. He takes another, glances again, then puts it in another basket. He moves rapidly though not fast enough to injure the chickens. The expert chicken sexer is at work.

The makings of the novelist are evident; Southall transforms his appointed news story of meagre story-telling potential into a visual, personalized narrative, decades before the New Journalism movement started using fictional techniques to tell journalistic stories.

Later, when he tried for a journalism cadetship and failed, Southall blamed his lack of education, a deficit that left him with a lifelong feeling of inferiority.

In 1941, at the age of twenty, Southall presented himself to the RAAF to enlist for active service. While waiting for his call-up, he was conscripted to the 22nd Field Regiment, and in December of 1941, following the Pearl Harbour bombing, was sent with a group of other conscripts to defend the Victorian coastline. For months, he alternated between lookout duty and resting in a cave shelter that the gunners had hollowed out from the foreshore scrub, an experience that later informed *Hills End*. Then one morning in 1942, Southall experienced something that would haunt him for the rest of his life. An Australian military aircraft came in from the sea and plunged violently into the ground. The impact and the blast, he says, "speared my heart like a splinter of ice that never thawed". Southall's comment is immediately reminiscent of Kafka's reflection on reading:

> we need books that affect us like a disaster, that grieve us deeply, like the death of someone we loved more than ourselves, like being banished into forests far from everyone, like a suicide …

Certainly Southall's disaster stories create this effect in their readers but this is exactly what bothered the critics. Should children be exposed to disasters of this magnitude? Should they read books that aggrieve them deeply? At one point in *Hills End*, the children find their beloved teacher lying at the bottom of a ravine, seemingly dead. And with each book that followed, the degree of trauma experienced by the child characters increased. In *Finn's Folly* (1969), a car accident leaves children orphaned alongside the corpses of their parents, causing one critic to suggest that the novel violated the *Children and Young Persons (Harmful Publications) Act*. And in the Carnegie Medal-winning *Josh* (1971), the young protagonist is so mentally tortured as to be diagnosed by one critic as "intensely paranoid", amounting to a literary experience of "constricted bitterness" and "fatalistic (if not nihilistic) suffering".

The story of *Josh* tells of the divide between city and country in Australia and between traditional primitive masculinity and an alternative masculinity of quiet intelligence. One critic described it as "an early example of the sensitive and vulnerable hero".

Even some of Southall's devoted readers wonder at the extent of pain he inflicted on his characters:

Ref 18-11-72

State School [illegible]
Bourchier St.
Shepparton 3630

Dear Mr. Southall,

I love your books and I think the best was Josh. Was Josh true? If it was I feel sorry for him. If it wasn't why did you make so much trouble for him?

Would you rather write for children or adults? What is your reason for your answer Is writing your favourite occupation? If not could you tell me your favourite hobby. I hope you will have time to answer.

Yours Sincerely
Giselle Hosgood

My impression is that Southall tested his boy characters to the very edge of endurance because it mirrored his own personal experience. Much of his writing seems to have its genesis in the death of his father and the son's subsequent resuming of responsibilities. Southall's books are populated again and again by young boys struck by disaster who are suddenly forced to become men. One critic, Paddy McCorry, suggests that most of Southall's books could be subtitled: "On Becoming a Man." Each novel is a portrait, in one way or another, of his own painful struggle with Australian masculinity.

Perhaps, in some small way, this is where I also identify with Southall – because I too have spent much of my life caught up in a struggle with Australian masculinity, first as a teenager on Cronulla beach, later with my mateship-obsessed husband, and more recently, as a witness to my son's dangerous journey into manhood.

* * *

On returning from his conscripted service on the Victorian coastline, Southall formally enlisted in the RAAF. After some initial training at Mornington Peninsula, he was sent to the Elementary Flying Training School in Benalla, Victoria. In 1942, he boarded a US troopship for a long journey that eventually ended at Pembroke in Wales, where the Second Australian Sunderland Squadron, No. 461, was based.

"The first operational flight was the hurdle," he writes in *They Shall Not Pass Unseen* (1956), a history of his squadron. "It stood up in front of you in a black gown with a scythe in hand ... A lot of squadrons were losing a lot of men ... It wasn't pleasant to arrive on a unit, strike up an acquaintance with the fellow in the next bunk, then look round for him blankly a few days later to learn that he was dead. He was too young to die, and so were you."

Every flight invoked terror. Fear was his principal opponent, he says, not the enemy. Fear and flying would also become two of the main themes of many of the books he was to write, including, and perhaps especially, *To the Wild Sky*.

* * *

It is said that all writing is an effort to find that which has been lost. I was nine when I devoted myself to the idea of being a writer. I was also nine when my father left home and my parents separated. Although the word "separate" wasn't articulated.

"Your father is moving to the city to be closer to his work," my mother explained. I accepted the explanation without question. My father's work was in Kensington, on the fourteenth floor of the School of Psychology building at the

University of New South Wales, a long way from our home in Kirrawee. Nevertheless, the house felt heavy with unspoken tension and emotion and I knew something momentous was happening. I also intuited that it was something beyond speaking about. And yet I yearned to have my say. So I picked up my pencil.

"I am sure that in nine out of ten cases the original wish to write is to make oneself felt," writes Elizabeth Bowen in a little book called *Why Do I Write?*. "It's a sign, I suppose, of life's decreasing livableness *as* life that people should feel it possible to make themselves felt in so few other ways."

V.S. Pritchett, in the same book, declares:

> When the inner history of any writer's mind is written, whatever his degree, we find (I believe) that there is a break at some point in his life. At some point he splits off from the people who surround him and he discovers the necessity of talking to himself and not to them. A monologue begins … To write is to be naïve, and one of the strange pleasures of the solitary monologue is the discovery that one has said aloud to oneself what other people are saying silently.

Perhaps this "splitting off" because of lost fathers is something that Southall and I have in common. The loss of my own father happened twice. Once when he left the family home and then again when he took his own life. I, too, had found much of my subject matter determined by an untimely death of a parent. I, too, had spent many of my writing hours re-living sudden tragedy and grappling with grief. I, too, had found catharsis in the writing process and looked for healing in the creation of narrative. Nevertheless, there are some scars that, no matter how carefully you write about them – in first, second, or third person; as fiction, essay, or confession – stubbornly refuse to heal.

On 19 October 1987, the stock market crashed worldwide. It was later to become known as Black Tuesday. My father, having spent his retirement secretly gambling his superannuation in share-trading, believed he was a ruined man. On his sixty-fourth birthday, eleven days after the birth of my first child, he hanged himself. I wrote a book about it, thinking this was the cure.

Thirty years later, now a writer, I feel a similar sense of ruin. But because my father chose suicide, I cannot. I understand too well the fallout for the family. So the exit strategy taken by Virginia Woolf, Sylvia Plath, Charlotte Perkins Gilman, and Helen Daniel is permanently closed. Perhaps the saying I had once heard many years ago was true: all writers are failed suicides.

* * *

The young photos of Ivan show a man with intensely searching, restless eyes. Snapshots of him smiling are rare. His serious nature was in part an inheritance of his strictly Methodist upbringing. Southall's father had wanted to be a missionary. Bible readings were *de rigour* after dinner every evening, and every Sunday revolved around the local Methodist church. Later in life, while living at Monbulk in the 1950s and 1960s, the local minister asked Ivan to help out with the circuit of congregations, and for a period he delivered sermons to schools and churches in the area. "In my stories from the pulpit I tell the epics of scripture in modern idiom", he writes. Perhaps his survival stories for children are also, in some form, sermons, and his readers, adoring and faithful, his congregation.

Every morning before he began to write, Ivan said a prayer. "He never lost his faith," his second wife, Susan, tells me, "although he may have lost faith in the church. He said his work was his prayer."

"I believe in what I'm doing or I wouldn't be doing it," writes Southall. "Without faith, I can see no reason for life nor any answers to the riddle of the world. All this would have no meaning."

How I envy such faith. Lack of it is at the very heart of my present predicament. If all writing is an effort to find that which has been lost, how do I go about finding my lost faith in writing itself? How do I write myself back into writing? How did Southall keep the faith? Can I blame my atheist upbringing for no longer believing that my words have meaning? What if I really can't write anymore? What will my life of devotion to the craft have been for?

Perhaps Southall's diligence in responding to his readers wasn't just an act of polite acknowledgement. Perhaps his direct relationship with them *was* the way he kept the faith. "The first thing he did every morning was go to the post office to collect his letters," his first wife, Joy, tells me. "Then he would spend the rest of the morning responding to them." Maybe he was just as dependent on his readers as they were on him. Perhaps without them he would have felt like a pastor preaching to an empty church.

* * *

Before travelling to Canberra to look at the Southall archives, I bought a signed first edition of *To the Wild Sky* from an antiquarian bookseller. I knew this was where I had to start – by re-reading the book that had determined my destiny. But I was so nervous about re-engaging with it as an adult that months went past and the book remained unopened. I was anxious about not being able to recall the excitement from fifty years ago, about the possibility that I'd lost the childish capacity for enchantment and about the real risk that I had fallen out of love with Ivan Southall.

After a week in the archives, I finally find the courage to open my copy of *To the Wild Sky*. For the first few chapters I withhold my critical mind, wanting and hoping for the feeling of enrapture to return, but by the fourth chapter my apprehension is confirmed. *I can't go back*. Even worse, I don't even believe that this award-winning book is particularly well written. The dialogue is clunky, the gender roles stereotyped, the grown-ups mostly mean-spirited and unlikeable and there is an uncomfortable obsession with class.

Bert is a typical Southall adult – rude and disrespectful to children:

> "Sit still," said Bert, "and keep your voice down. I can't stand shriekin' kids. If you want to ride in a taxi with grown-ups behave like one."
>
> Bert moved off and squinted at the boy. "Don't pick your friends from the toffee-noses, do you?" Bert knew he was a Hennessy, of a long line of Hennessys. Bert himself was a working man – or called himself one – with no great love of the Squatting Class … "Does Dad approve of your

> friends, kid? Takin' them home to the baronial hall?"

Jim, the short-lived pilot of the light plane, is not much better.

> Jim could see what was going on, but was too impatient, too frustrated, to work out the reasons for it. All he could feel was an intense annoyance, an intense disappointment in the *quality* of the children.

I have not just fallen out of love with my childhood literary hero. Worse than that, I am filled with a palpable *dislike.*

But then I thought, as I always do when there seems to be something wrong with the world: is the real problem that there is something wrong with me? Have I perhaps *turned into* one of those mean-spirited adults? Transformed from the adoring reader to the purse-lipped critic. Maybe I am just simply out of touch with my inner child. Because this was Southall's magic: he could imagine himself back into childhood. And this was the problem with the adults in his novels: that they could not: "Like Bert, [Jim] too had forgotten what it was like to be a boy."

This was why Southall readers loved him so. He spoke to them directly, as equals. He was an adult who remembered what it was like and who was *on their side.*

I decide to return to the Reading Room of the National Library and look again at the correspondence, determined to find a way to rekindle my love for Southall the person, if not the writer.

Where I find Southall most admirable is in his responses to pieces of prose and poetry that children send in for his opinion, all of which, in my view, demonstrate not a shred of literary merit. He shows a generosity of spirit and a patience that I realise I have been lacking in my re-reading of *To the Wild Sky.*

In 1969, a reader from Minnesota sends poems, one based on *Ash Road* and another on *To the Wild Sky*:

Once there were some boys.
That did not have no toys
But when their houses burn, it made a lot of noise.
Once there was a boy
Who knew how to fly
Over 2000 feet in the sky.
The boys and girls were
Eating pie as they watched
The objects go by.

Please write back and tell me what you think and how I can improve it.

Dear Laurie,

Thank you for your poems. Keep writing them; that's the way to improve them. The more often you write the better you become. Write about things that happen to yourself; things that happen to you every day because there is a poem in everything that happens to us only if we take time to think about it long enough.

Ivan Southall

Southall replies to the inane as well as the intelligent, patiently supplying information for school projects on Australian authors and book reviews, often answering the same lists of questions over and over.

Jennifer writes from Beverley Hills Primary School that:

as a member of Grade 6B, I have been asked, as part of an English project, to conduct an interview by mail, to an important Australian personality. I have chosen you. Would you please be kind enough to answer the following questions?

1. *Where were you born?*
2. *Where did you go to primary school?*
3. *Where did you go to secondary school?*
4. *Did you like school? If you didn't, why not?*
5. *What was your favourite subject at school?*
6. *What was your worst subject at school?*
7. *How did you start your career?*
8. *Did any particular person help you in your early stages?*
9. *Do you have any brothers or sisters?*
10. *What has been the most exciting moment in your life?*
11. *What has been your most popular book?*
12. *Have you won any awards? If so, how many what are they?*
13. *Do you have any pets? If so, how many and what are they?*
14. *If possible may I have an autographed photo please?*

The first thing that strikes me about this letter is that a sixth-grader considered a writer to be "an important Australian personality". My growing sense of the writing vocation as useless and unproductive in comparison to nursing or even landscape gardening is integral to my late-life crisis. It is hard to maintain one's sense of self-value if your product, so to speak, is not in any way necessary for society to function. So it's nice to know that in 1972 Jennifer believed that Southall was "an important Australian".

Dear Jennifer,

Fourteen questions to answer! Well, here goes . . .

In the evening, I return to my half-read copy of *To the Wild Sky,* determined to get to the end.

What grates most are the comments about girls:

"Danger?" squealed Stevie. That was a word for women.

"Gee whiz. Do they think you're a girl or somethin'?"

"Am I to be plagued all day by a bunch of hysterical females?"

> Girls were different from boys. Having girls around was like being trapped in a bear pit.

But it's not just these asides that, after all, only reflect the era. It's that the boys get to be deep and thoughtful as they undergo their teenage inner turmoils while girls remain on the periphery of any action, physical or emotional: exactly the reason why I had grown up feeling resentful about being a woman.

I am relieved then, and find myself softening to my old literary hero, when on the last page of *To the Wild Sky,* Southall allows Jan to light the fire, the only hope of survival for this hungry, bedraggled group of lost children.

> Suddenly flames came … handfuls of flames that Jan, shrieking with excitement, pushed into her fireplace … And Jan, exhausted, lapsed into a smile of something like bliss.
>
> The fire leapt up, crackling, with a warm glow and flickering shadows and showers of sparks and bright smoke, just like an ordinary camp-fire that might burn in that other world where friends and families lived far away. It immediately brought

> that world so much closer, immediately made it real again. And for the very first time, Jan found herself hoping that the people looking for them didn't find them too soon, for really and truly there were so many things it would be fun to do.

Perhaps this was what I found appealing – a young girl who is lost and yet hopes not to be rescued "too soon" because danger, she understands intuitively, is an essential part of fun.

Even as a child I had felt the attraction of a fun edged with danger. I had discovered it in my own habit of playing with matches in the bushland bordering our suburban back yard. And I often threatened my mother with running away, keen to seek out risk, yearning for a fire of baptism that would deliver me into the wondrous world of adulthood. I was Jan and Jan was me.

Had this heroine been the reason for my childish belief in this book? Because I had believed, utterly. Indeed, my future had been almost entirely determined by the power of this story and the conviction that I could survive – bravely and courageously – even if marooned on a remote island. But now I am no longer a believer. After a lifetime of crashing and burning, playing at bravery and resilience, I find myself shipwrecked. Yes, as Jan says, there were "so many things" it was fun to do, but, also like Jan, I did want to be rescued eventually. And here I am, at sixty, still waiting.

The man who had once been the turning point of my life, with whom I'd had a secret and intimate relationship – ("like a love affair", as Southall put it in an essay about the reader-writer relationship) no longer holds any attraction. And I start to wonder, in the same way I wonder about ex-boyfriends and former husbands: *What did I ever see in him?*

As was usual with Southall, the critics were divided about *To the Wild Sky.* Dennis Hall, reviewing for the *Australian Book Review*, claimed that it was the most ambitious children's book so far attempted by an Australian writer. Others believed the book was too dark, with one critic accusing Southall of borrowing from *Lord of the Flies*. When *To the Wild Sky* won the Children's Book Council Award, Brenda Niall stated that she thought it would have been more appropriate for him to have been awarded the "William Golding Prize for Cultural Pessimism". But what bothers critics and readers alike is the unresolved ending. Would the children be rescued or would they be left on this lone island forever?

In 1968, a young boy writes to Southall to articulate a common complaint:

Dear Mr Southall — 36 Timms Ave, Croydon 3136

I have just finished reading your book, To The Wild Sky I enjoyed the story very much but I'm very disappointed with the ending why did you write a ending like that? Now I don't know if they were rescued, or if they died, or if they ~~tived~~ lived there for the rest of their lives.

sincerely
Andrew Jay

And Susan felt the same:

> *I'm still quite cross about the way you let us work out what happens in To the Wild Sky but I hope that the children were found.*

In 1969, Southall responds to Richard, yet another reader yearning for a "proper ending":

Dear Richard,

I am very happy you are reading my books even if you are finding the endings a little difficult at times. Writers have a habit of doing this sort of thing, you know. We don't always like telling you everything that happens. We like to leave a little to your own imagination so that you might go on thinking about what you have read. In real life we hardly ever know everything about anything, and in stories, when a writer is honest, he knows he must not tie everything up in a neat bundle with all the answers given because his readers might start expecting real life to give them all the answers all the time and one of the most exciting things about being alive is always to be wondering, "What will happen next?"

"*To the Wild Sky* grew out of day dreams I had as a boy," says Southall in 1968, "– of flying an aeroplane far away to a wonderful place where no-one would ever find me." Is this why he leaves the children abandoned on the island? Is he living out his childhood fantasy?

Another reader writes from Bethlehem College, Ashfield, in 1970:

Why did you leave To the Wild Sky unfinished? You introduce thoughts of death frequently. Why?

Southall's response is frank and open, as he always is in his letters to admirers:

A book is a very personal thing, particularly when it is about believable people in a situation of real life. I was not really aware that death played a prominent part in my books. Looking back, I can see this. Death does come up again and again, but of course death is part of living.

My view is that the open-ended finale of *To the Wild Sky* appeals to the creative mind, which is naturally risk-taking, to the child who can imagine her own ending, who considers the openness as an invitation, from the master to the novice, to write her own vision in her own words. And it was an invitation that I couldn't resist, not knowing, as I do now, what dark and difficult navigations lay ahead. At that age, it was precisely the darkness, the clouds of unknowing, that I found alluring. But the truth is that Southall set me on a flighty career with no navigation tools and no happy ending. And now I feel betrayed. I was only a child after all.

* * *

"Twelve hours a day it might hold me for a week or two weeks or more, just looking for the door, with little to show, but I have learnt not to rush, not to push hard until the moment is there," writes Southall in an essay called "Something Like a Love Affair":

> And then, "Eureka." The door! It opens. A mood, a word, a certainty that from here I go on into the unknown, that inexhaustible source of originalities from out of which comes excitement that I wish all could enjoy. The unknown is a word ahead of me all the time, word by word I move out into it, a patient, wondering, questing exploration. A contemplation of the word.

Although Southall vowed not to write a sequel to *To the Wild Sky*, many years later he succumbed to pressure and wrote *A City out of Sight*, published in 1984. But by that time, frustrated readers like Andrew and Susan would have been in their twenties and unlikely to be interested in the fates of Gerald, Carol, Colin, Bruce, and Jan. And in any case, it seems that Southall didn't really believe in the project. The Author's Note reads:

> I have always held the view that readers might have their own expectations and might enjoy living them out in their imaginations. At heart, I have not changed my position, but I have agreed to go on with the story.

If he didn't believe in it, why did he write it? Was he relenting to publisher and reader pressure? Or perhaps it was simply necessity, forced upon him by the fiscal reality of being a professional writer.

* * *

I find myself compelled to seek out more details of Southall's personal life, in an effort to understand the person behind the books.

After the war, Southall returned to London to take up his first full-time job as a writer, compiling a history of his squadron,

Number 461, otherwise known as the Anzac Squadron. He worked writing military history by day and fiction by night on his new Corona Special typewriter in his very own office of the RAAF Overseas Headquarters. Also working there was a young filing clerk by the name of Joy Blackburn. She had previously had two other Australian boyfriends, both pilots, but neither had survived the war.

Ivan and Joy first met in 1945 under circumstances that were perhaps prophetic of what was to come. They had barely exchanged names when Ivan observed: "I think you dropped something." Joy looked down and saw that her brand new *crêpe-de-chine* cami-knickers had fallen around her ankles. "So I have," she said, and quickly pulled them up and left the room. Sixty years later, Ivan was to reflect: "Our subsequent relationship became a tale of immoderate beginnings and endings."

At the age of twenty-four, after six months of courtship, Ivan proposed and the couple moved into a flat near the West End. Here, Southall began to have some success selling stories to *Woman's Own.* By the beginning of 1946, his output was impressive: two books, twenty-one short stories, six articles, and one poem. His writing timetable was strict: "I work a set number of hours for three days in the week, and find that that period is sufficient to leisurely produce about 3,500 words." But finding publishers wasn't easy. By that time he had only eight acceptances and fifty-seven rejection slips.

The first rumblings of marital discontent began to appear when Ivan wanted to spend his weekends at his desk rather than with his new wife. "If I can't stay at home to write, I'll go away to write," he told her.

Like so many writers, Southall was *driven*, often to the detriment of his personal relationships. This is something I can relate to, having repeatedly failed in my attempts to combine motherhood, marriage, *and* writing. Something has to be sacrificed, and it is never the writing. But now I am thinking that my priorities are a mistake. Writing, after all, is not a pleasure-seeking exercise; it is solitary, anti-social, and rarely profitable; a practice that a person would only persevere with if she really had to.

As Southall writes to one of the many would-be authors who sought out his advice on the pursuit of a writing career:

> *The only way I can write these days is to go away but this means I have to be very lonely because I must go on my own. Sometimes that is all right; it depends upon your mood; sometimes it is very difficult. The person who writes stories is usually born to write and can't help himself. He has GOT to write. If that's the way it is with you, that's the way it will be.*

If Southall is right, perhaps questioning my vocation is as useful as questioning my nationality or my gender, and being a writer is not a matter of faith, as I had thought, but of fate. And yet, being a male writer is fundamentally different to being a female writer. Going away to write must have been lonely for Southall but he seems to forget that his very ability to go away – his unquestioned freedom to abandon his wife and family – was in fact a privilege most women writers only dream of having.

Six months after Ivan and Joy married, the couple embarked for Australia. They moved into Ivan's childhood home in Surrey Hills, a suburb of Melbourne, Victoria. By this time, Joy was pregnant. Southall returned to the Melbourne *Herald* to finish the process engraver apprenticeship he had started prior to the war, turning down a suggestion from his employer that he might be better suited to the literary staff. Southall was determined to develop his career as an independent writer. He believed that, having been lucky enough to return from the war alive, he owed it to himself to live out his dream, which he imagined spending "largely in solitude upon a modest writing surface [with] a stack of unmarked quarto paper."

In March 1947, Joy gave birth to a son, Andrew. Southall was not present for his son's birth and, according to his biographer Stephanie Steggall, "recorded it unemotionally in his diary of 1947."

In November of that year, Southall left the *Herald* offices amid murmurings from workmates that he would regret his decision. But Joy joined her husband in his idealism, excited about the prospect of being a writer's wife. Under a housing scheme for selected ex-servicemen, they moved with their firstborn into a new home in Brighton. The friction that was to characterise their marriage, however, continued. Southall was perturbed by the newborn's interruption of his writing schedule, while Joy was homesick and longing for attention from her husband.

As a freelance writer, Southall was smart enough to know that he needed a basic weekly income to supplement his vocation, so he bought a motor mower and began the Kingsway Lawn Service. His biographer notes that by July 1948, Southall "was cutting grass four and a half days and spending less time at the typewriter. He began to wonder seriously if it was impossible to be a writer in Australia, just as everyone had warned him." The after-effects of war didn't help. Southall was hospitalised several times for a nervous condition, probably post-traumatic stress disorder. He would suffer from "war nerves" for the rest of his life: unable to cope with slamming doors or raised voices and having repetitive nightmares about his house being blown away or falling down.

Southall remained restless and decided to pursue his old romantic notion of a country retreat, where he imagined he could write in perfect peace. The couple found a property, Blackwood Farm, on Old Emerald Road, a couple of miles out from Monbulk in the foothills of the Dandenong Ranges.

"There opened this sublime view of valleys and mountains and blueness and immensity and openness and freedom," Southall writes. "There was this little bush shack made out of hand-cut timbers on bush stumps. Locked, so we couldn't get into it. I said, 'This has got to be it,' and so we paid five pounds deposit, which was all we had." He set to work to build a house for his family "largely from the components of old hen houses and sheds".

The move to Blackwood Farm coincided with the publication of *Meet Simon Black* (1950), the first of the Simon Black series that would provide the part-time writer, part-time farmer with a small but steady income for the next decade. Southall was at last on the road to becoming a professional writer. However, the romantic notion of retreating to the country eventually brought disillusion. The French beans were eaten by rabbits, the horse pulled up the raspberry crop, the foxes destroyed the hens, the frost killed the lemon trees, and a record cold winter finished off the passionfruit.

While Southall's crops failed, his family grew. A daughter, Roberta, was born in 1950, and another, Elizabeth, in 1959. But his children were not his focus. While busily writing to and for his thousands of child fans, Southall's own children were locked out of his study and, largely, out of his life.

His son, Andrew, who prefers to be known as Drew, describes their life at Blackwood Farm and the rules in relation to the study, which was situated in the garden at a distance from the hubbub of the family home: "You didn't go near his study, even on weekends. You didn't make a noise in or around the study. You weren't *seen* through the windows of the study. At the back door of the house, there was a bell. If the children caused a problem, my mother would ring the bell. In the end, she only had to threaten to ring the bell because the consequences were so awful. He was just a bloody disciplinarian."

The father of three was not to be disturbed between the hours of 8am to 6pm. At 6pm, he would emerge for dinner. Drew recalls: "He'd come out of the study and spend an hour with the family. I remember all the kids would be sitting around chatting with Mum, and then Dad would come in and it would all stop. All that rah-rah around the kitchen. Dad would come in the door and it would all stop … After dinner, all the children got sent to bed so my mother could get some time with Dad before he went back to the study. Summer or winter, we were sent to bed at 6:30. That was something I really resented … Mum basically brought us up. I can't say Dad had anything to do with bringing us up, apart from putting a roof over our heads. I said to my sister that I used to wish that my father would beat me up because at least it would have been contact."

Drew also felt out of place with his peers in the local rural town of Monbulk, where his friends were all sons of tradesmen, timber cutters, or factory hands: "The feeling I got around the school yard was that my father was a lazy bastard, and why didn't he have a real job in the sawmill or jam factory like nearly all the other kids' parents did? That is what I felt too … I stood out, mainly because of my father but also because my mother was English. And we were dumped into this subsistence farming community of mill workers and jam producers and I ended up wanting to be like those people."

The fact that money was so scarce also increased the family tension: "It was subsistence living. At least the other kids' parents had a regular income, which we never did. Except when Dad was doing deliveries to the Queen Victoria market … I never got pocket money. The only way I earned money was by getting the firewood. I gathered it in an old wheelbarrow with a steel wheel and was paid a penny per barrow load. Without a rubber tyre. For a fuckin' penny … I had friends whose dads weren't necessarily good role models either but they were dads, and the only people I remember getting along with were the mothers of those boys, because they were accessible. They gave me time without wanting me to plough a paddock or hoe strawberries or cut the firewood."

Many years later, Ivan Southall described some of the daily privations of Blackwood Farm: drought, carrying water in buckets four hundred yards, shade temperatures of up to one-hundred-and-twelve, kerosene lamps blowing up, deadly snakes in the roof, children caught between the floorboard joists under the house, and no telephone to call for help. "My father had his heartbreaks," writes Southall. "Blackwood Farm was one of mine. My Eden, but my heartbreak."

When his editor Beatrice Davis expressed concern about one of Angus and Robertson's most important authors living a hand-to-mouth existence, the salaried sales manager, Bill Hughes, had no sympathy. He responded to Southall's grievance letter about late royalty statements with the comment: "He chose to be an author and if the conditions do not suit him he should consider a change of career."

"No wonder they can't find the Australian author," Southall retorted in his journal. "If he has not gone into radio or advertising or overseas, he has starved to death."

Ivan's fourth child was due on his fortieth birthday, 8 June 1961, but Joy went into labour two weeks early. The baby girl was quickly taken by ambulance to be "checked" at the Royal Children's Hospital in Melbourne. That evening, the parents were informed that Melissa had Down syndrome. Of all the trials in Southall's life, this was possibly the most painful.

In that same year, Drew Southall left home: "I was so happy to get out. I lived with a mortal fear of my father ever finding out about what I'd done wrong. And that were lots of things that I had done wrong. My mother thinks I left home because of Melissa, but I didn't. I left home because of them. I hated having to go to church on Sundays. I hated having to wear short pants. And as a kid, I hated my father."

Drew may have been able to find his freedom by leaving the family home but for Joy there was no such easy solution. She had abandoned her country and her family for the love of a young Australian writer but now she felt completely isolated. Without a telephone or neighbours, Joy was a constant witness to her husband's long-distance relationship with his readers, as well as the all-consuming relationship with his own mind.

I am beginning to think that the only thing worse than being a writer is being a writer's spouse. Or perhaps being a writer's child. How was it possible that this man could speak to hundreds of thousands of his young readers, spend every morning writing so tenderly to his devoted audience, and yet not spend time with to his very own children?

But I know the answer. Because my father was the same. And possibly, so am I. I have also found myself, at times, more devoted to my writing than to my children. Once, while on a writers' retreat I received a call from my son saying he was having an anxiety attack; he was starting a new job and he was in a panic, unable to breathe. I told him to take a Valium and that I would be back in a week. Well, not in those words, but in effect. I refused to give up my retreat. Like Ivan, I wanted my child kept at a distance so I could concentrate. I wonder now if this writing vocation is more like an addiction. We feel an overwhelming compulsion that trumps all other needs; we are absolutely incapable of resisting it, just as an addict is helpless before her drug. Perhaps I've spent my entire life hooked. "For when the fiction drug is pure," says novelist Tim Parks, "inebriation is guaranteed. This is not an easy habit to break."

* * *

In 1962, drought came to Blackwood Farm and then a bushfire threatened the property, forcing the family to flee and take refuge in a potato paddock. By then, Joy had lost any romantic illusions about being married to a writer amid the beauty of the Australian bushland. "Joy wanted me to call quits at the desk," writes Southall. "To leave at eight each morning and return at six and bring in a weekly pay cheque. Life was too stressed. The income too small. The isolation, after twelve years, really getting to her … Our family had grown … They had to be fed, clothed and educated."

Then in 1963, Southall finally received a royalty cheque he wouldn't complain about. *Hills End* was paying off and the writer proudly commented that he was getting "the returns of oil shares". After thirteen years, the decision was made to abandon the farm. The family moved into a newly built home at the Patch, Victoria, that Southall named Hills End, in celebration of his hard-won success. But the work of writing wasn't getting any easier. "Plagued by boils and chronic tiredness," writes his biographer, "he had been perturbed that writing had become harder and harder."

Southall embarked on a number of non-fiction works, including a biography of a pioneering Methodist missionary in Arnhem Land, but after producing thousands of words, nothing came to fruition. Afterwards, his attempt at comedy didn't impress Beatrice Davis. Then, late in 1964, he regained his confidence as he began writing *Ash Road.*

* * *

One theory about writers is that they are so terrified of life that instead of dealing with the real world, they turn everything into a metaphor. Everything becomes mediated, and by having reality mediated, they are protected from raw reality. Or, as Martin Amis says in *The Information,* his famous book about literary rivalry, "Why does the writer keep writing? To avoid facing up to naked, unmitigated, unmediated reality." The original reason for a writer's terror, it is theorised, is some deep trauma from childhood. Then as they grow up, writing becomes a way of dealing with fears of an adult kind as well.

I realise now that in my own life I have used writing to try to create a force field around me, as well as a healing force to assuage wounds. All writing is about loss, says the great Irish short story writer, Claire Keegan, and all writing is the act of writing into that loss. Ivan wrote into the loss of his father; I wrote into the loss of mine. Then I wrote into the loss of my mother, my sister, my brother and my son.

If it's true that writers write in order to manage their fears, it would have come naturally to Southall to take the trauma of the bushfire that threatened his home and family and transform it into *Ash Road.* And this time the writing into loss paid off. After so many years of exhausting work, both at his desk and on the farm, Southall finally achieved the recognition in Australia that he yearned for. In 1966, *Ash Road* won the Children's Book Council's Book of the Year Award and marked the beginning of the Southall phenomenon and a decade of celebrity author status. Writing to his editor, Beatrice Davis, he confessed: "I have hopes that rather than having entered my 'prime' I may only be just beginning and that everything else has been part of the apprenticeship."

The fan letters poured in, many strongly identifying with the characters of *Ash Road*:

> *Dear Mr Southall,*
>
> *Sister's family was burnt out twice but she didn't see it happen. She knows a man just like Grandpa Tanner.*

> *Dear Mr Southall,*
>
> *I felt the same as Peter when he left childhood behind.*
>
> *Mark*

Dear Mr Southall,

Were the children in the book real children you had known or were they cousins of your children or were they your own children?

Maureen

Southall had discovered his true talent: the ability to write books in which his young readers could recognise themselves, a pleasure that he had sorely missed while growing up. "Childhood in the twenties and thirties was a comic culture," Southall writes, "an alien culture … the products of overworked hack writers." The only books Southall read as a child – "over and over and over again" – depicted settings and situations that were foreign to him. "In any situation I read about I could see myself only by suspending belief in myself."

Writing the survival stories was a way for Southall to believe in himself, a need that relates to another theory about the psychology of writers – that they have a very poor sense of self and that the only way they can believe in themselves is by creating written reflections that confirm their existence. "Did you ever read about a completely believable boy or girl who spoke your language and thought your thoughts and had your problems and experienced your fears?" Southall asks. "If you were an Australian in my day I am all but certain you could not."

Southall may have written out of a need to confirm his own sense of self in the world, but his stories also answered a need felt by others growing up in Australia at that time. For many young people, reading Southall's survival stories was the first experience of a convincing story set in their own country. This was also what struck me upon reading *To the Wild Sky* following the French fable of *The Little Prince* and the very British *Coral Island.*

Another writer-to-be, John Marsden, liked the Southall stories because "they were Australian and they were about the bush mostly and they were real. Real kids doing real stuff."

The Director General of the National Library of Australia, Marie-Louise Ayres, distinctly remembers reading *Ash Road.* "It was the first time I had realised that Australia was a place where fiction could happen," she says.

And for Malcolm Allbrook, of the Centre of Biography at the Australian National University, *Ash Road* was key to his assimilation into Australian society after arriving from Uganda as a child. "The first day we arrived we went to the beach and all the kids had sunburnt noses with pink zinc on them and they were screeching in a language I just didn't understand. I'd come from a colonial culture of 'How do you do?' and 'Beg your pardon?' so when *Ash Road* came my way I devoured it. It helped me understand about the history of Australia, and Australian society, and particularly country Australia".

* * *

Writing realism for Southall's particular target audience – ten to thirteen year olds – is still recognised by contemporary children's authors as one of the most difficult of genres. In order for the children to have agency, the adults need to be absent, but creating a plausible situation where this might happen, especially in these days of hover-parents, is not easy. "It's a very under-appreciated art – what Southall did," says young adult novelist Kirsty Murray. "Getting rid of the adults is very difficult. Even now, if you look across any particular year, it's actually a very small proportion of books that are doing what Southall did. And when you get it right, it really hits home."

Clearly, Southall was ahead of his time – the term "young adult fiction" was yet to be invented – but as usual, there were critics who thought his realism went too far, commenting on the "severity" of the story and the concern that *Ash Road* could have a negative effect on children's nerves.

Perhaps this is something else that Southall and I share. My first, co-authored book is a young adult novel that was also criticised for being shocking and unfit for young people to read. *Puberty Blues* (1979) is also an attempt to write realistically – about real teenagers going through real life events. The big difference is that I write autobiographically, while Southall is careful to maintain the safety screen of fiction, even though *Ash Road* is so clearly the result of personal experience. This is a lesson I wish I had learnt as a young writer. There are some stories that are too painful for the first person pronoun and should only be told through the protective shroud of fiction.

Yet for some Southall readers, his works, no matter how fictionalised, still retain the sting of raw personal wounds. Although Southall didn't publish memoir, there is a sense of self-revelation in his books that critic Walter McVitty finds particularly unnerving:

> So personal and candid has the writing been in each [book] that one might describe the process ... as undressing in public. Although private doubts, fears and phobias, feelings of inadequacy, failure and alienation are being admitted and laid bare, they are feelings with which most of us can identify. Obviously this confessional quality explains why Ivan Southall's novels strike a sympathetic chord in some readers, but just as obviously it helps explain why other readers feel distinctly uncomfortable and irritated (if not embarrassed) by them.

Is this why Southall makes me feel uncomfortable? Because, as a confessional writer, there is something that Ivan Southall and I have in common? Perhaps my discomfort is really the discomfort of self-recognition. And if so, why do I find the reflection of myself so difficult to contemplate? Maybe the reason I no longer love Ivan the writer is because I no longer love the writer in myself.

* * *

Ash Road was followed by *To the Wild Sky,* which again won the Children's Book Council Book of the Year Award in 1968. Rather than take the occasion to celebrate, Southall used the awards ceremony to address his critics in person, describing them as a brutal and bloodied boundary between the writer and the reader:

> Beyond the writer, between him and the child, has grown a barbed wire entanglement through which his book, beating with his own blood, must thrust its way … You people here represent the citadel of enlightened adult opinion … that the writer of serious intent for children in this country must eventually conquer … Critics have flogged me up and down the village square for

> eighteen years … The writing of a book, however ill-conceived, is a labour at least of months; the writing of criticism is rarely the labour of more than a few days.

This is a side of Southall I find hard to warm to. I can well understand how wounding criticism can be, but surely an award is an occasion for celebration rather than airing grievances. The speech, though sincere, reveals an inability to withstand criticism of almost any kind and a Puritan-style rigidity and righteousness. Indeed, the tone sounds suspiciously like one of the persecuted, misunderstood young men in Southall's novels. Adults, perhaps, were the enemy for Southall, not just in his novels, but also in real life. Maybe this explains the extraordinary closeness he developed with his young readers. They were his true kindred spirits, the pure souls uncorrupted by criticism or adult prejudice. Perhaps it was only in the correspondence with his readers that Ivan Southall felt truly understood.

Joy Southall remembers attending one of the many public events at which her husband spoke. A member of the audience commented, "Oh, your children must be so proud of you." Ivan responded: "You would have to ask my wife about that." "Fortunately they didn't," says Joy, "because the reality is that Robbie and Drew stayed away from him as much as they could.

Ivan couldn't show affection with his two eldest children, only with Elizabeth and sometimes Melissa."

"He didn't really engage with me as a dad," says Drew. "It was only when I started to work professionally in my early twenties that I started to value my father. Up until that point, I wouldn't have cared if he lived or died. Even then, what I felt was a respect for what my father did – his work – not exactly respect for him."

This was perhaps the only way that Southall could engage with his family – through writing, as a professional. His emotions were so huge that they needed to be worked through via the act of writing. In that way, the maelstrom of feelings, so often portrayed through painful, visceral scenes in his novels involving young tortured men, could be tamed and shaped and made sense of. Again, I too am guilty. All my life I have written about family, often to communicate things to my children that I cannot bring myself to say in person. Upon reading my books, my daughter often responds: "I didn't know you felt like that." Or, "You didn't tell me that was what happened," or "That's the first time I've heard about …

a) why you separated from my father
b) how grandpa died
c) the reason you became a writer.

* * *

In 1967 Southall began working on *Let the Balloon Go*, about a young polio victim, in part as a way of trying to come to terms with living with his own severely disabled daughter. Set on a single day, the protagonist, John Clement Sumner, triumphs in the final pages by climbing a tree. Southall was again pushing boundaries and some critics questioned his decision to put a "spastic" at the centre of his novel. But children continued to write to the author to express their appreciation:

> *Dear Mr Southall,*
>
> *We have just read your story Let the Balloon Go. We all thought it was so good the way you put the expression into it. The story was so good it made me think it was really happening and I was watching it happen. I think it was so good I just don't no what to write but I really think it was good.*
>
> *Love, Hazel*
>
> *Please write soon.*

> *Dear Mr Southall,*
>
> *I have just finished reading Let the Balloon Go for the sixth time.*
>
> *Christeen*

Mark Muus
Bayswater State
School 10-7-72 3135

Dear Mr Southall
Mr Tarran read us a story called Let the Balloon Go and it took about 3 weeks to finsh. Mr Tarran made some real good jokes and the best part was when he said Hi sun! Hi wind! Hi clouds! When we finshed the book. Mr Tarran went to the Library and got another of your books called the fox hole and it was a real groovy book and the best part was when he got stuck in the gully and he sunk the Chinamans shaft and he said "Theses gold down here" and his friends came down and said that they must get Ken up— that was the end of the story so make an ending for it please.

Love
From
Mark

RS 27.7.72

Mark is quoting directly from the book. As the disabled John climbs higher in the tree, he calls out to the sun and wind and clouds, a cry of freedom. At the centre of all Southall's striving – of any writer's striving – is always the cry of freedom, that strange, sometimes self-destructive urge to fly away to an unknown island with nothing but your own wondrous and awful being.

* * *

In the 1970s, Southall entered a new period that Agnes Nieuwenhuizen describes as "a phase depicting the inner struggles of boys who were 'different' or trapped within themselves. Highly intelligent, sensitive, introspective *internally* articulate boys struggle to overcome often imaginary but none the less 'real' fears and hurdles."

Michael Cameron, at the centre of Southall's novel *Bread and Honey* (1970), resonated with many young Australian readers of the 1970s, as the correspondence shows:

> *Dear Mr Southall,*
>
> *I felt sorry for Michael because of his mother's death and because he didn't accept himself as he was. I'm glad he realised in the end that nobody can change him and it's no good trying to be different*

from what you really are just to please other people.

Sue

There is, however, one reader who offers a criticism:

I thought Michael thought too much and didn't speak enough.

This is an accusation that could probably have been levelled at Ivan Southall himself. He wasn't a typical Aussie bloke. He didn't hang round bars drinking beers and exchanging banter. If friends visited his house, they were mostly writers or editors. He wasn't one for socialising. He spent most of his life thinking or writing in silence. In a sense, his books from this period can be seen as reflecting his continuing struggle with conventional Australian masculinity.

Jenny Pausacker's view is that Southall is one of the few writers who "lets us in on what it's like to be a bloke":

I do think the whole process of deciding whether to be a full-on guy, a full-on girl or a gender resister of one kind or another is bound to be stressful. Most of us stop stressing at some point but perhaps Southall never did, making him both atypical and a good informant.

Bread and Honey is set on Anzac Day, the Australian day for celebrating mateship. Despite being a decorated veteran, Southall didn't take part in marching or drinking with old war buddies. Even as an old man, there was something of the introspective, internally articulate boy who, like Michael in *Bread and Honey*, felt out of place with "real" Australian men. I suspect that if I'd met Southall in person, this is an aspect of his personality I would have warmed to: the emotional, over-sensitive, slightly tortured soul; the gentle man in a world of boofy blokes.

So why was being a male such a struggle for Southall? He was competent in so many ways, including most of the traditional masculine physical competencies. He could build houses, landscape gardens, run a lawn-mowing business, not to mention pilot flying boats. He could support a wife and four children. And he was also competent creatively and intellectually, publishing a total of fifty-three books. Despite his lifelong doubts, Southall demonstrated all the masculine traits I admire, including the virtue I cherish above all: courage.

During the war, Southall said that fear was his greatest enemy. But he faced up to that fear. And being able to face up to fears, another traditionally masculine virtue, was what he wanted to teach his young readers to do. Although he was incensed by comments from literary critics, who believed his stories exposed children to too much suffering, Southall never wavered from his belief in the kind of writer he thought he was destined to be. He wanted to teach children about dealing with disappointment, about resilience and managing adversity. Most of all, he wanted to teach them courage.

* * *

By 1974, Southall's marriage, which had always been stormy, reached a crisis point. Although he understood that his own behaviour had caused much of Joy's unhappiness, Ivan believed that his wife "never let up" and felt "that he had endured a form of domestic violence". The difficulties of caring for Melissa, their disabled child, also contributed to pushing their relationship over the edge. But the real reason for the final break in the marriage was that Ivan had fallen in love.

In 1971, during Southall's trip to the United States he met Susan Stanton, then thirty-four and also married, who had been given the job of minding the famous Australian writer during his visit to the University of California, Berkeley.

Susan was a graduate of the University and part of the alternative counter-culture of the time. She practised tarot card reading, held séances and read Carl Jung. On his return to

Australia, Southall and Susan became regular correspondents and Southall went back to the US to see her again in 1974, the same year he proposed a separation from Joy.

"I remember the day when there was a knock at the door and my mother was standing there," says Drew. "Dad had just told her about Susan. That was it. It was over. She wanted me to talk to him so I drove up to the Patch with a bottle of red wine between my legs, which I drank the whole way up there. I went in and he told me all about Susan." He adds: "I think on some level my mother blames me. She thinks he copied my promiscuous behaviour."

In December 1974, the couple agreed to a trial separation. The anxiety of the break-up immediately poured into the novel *What About Tomorrow?* (1977), in which another highly anxious teenage boy runs away from home:

> Where to? Oh, where to now? Heaven knew. Along the centre of the road, along the crown, wavering along by instinct, by instinct steering his way, seeing not a living soul. It was the longest night in the history of the world.

How well he captures the nightmarish ache of a break-up, the terror of being utterly alone, the melancholy dark night of the soul, and its accompanying corrosive fear that you may never wake to the bright world again. But of course, he wasn't just running away from a suffocating marriage; he was running towards what he believed to be his artistic freedom. "When he went away he wrote a letter saying he had decided not to come back to the family," says Joy, "– not just me – *the family*. And he wanted to leave so that he could write."

By mid-1975, Susan had left her husband and travelled to Sydney to be with Ivan. "I will marry her as soon as I am legally able to," Southall told his friend and fellow writer, Maurice Saxby. Southall's decision to re-marry so quickly made a difficult divorce even more bitter: "I know he felt ashamed," says Joy. "He'd grown up in a strict Methodist house with very strong ideas about what was right. He knew what he'd done wasn't right."

Elizabeth Bowen believes that writers aren't really capable of real-world relationships. In a letter to a fellow writer, she explains:

> *Perhaps one emotional reason why one may write is the need to work off, out of the system, the sense of being solitary and farouche. Solitary and farouche people don't have relationships; they are quite unrelatable. If you and I were capable of being altogether house-trained and made jolly, we should be nicer people, but not writers ... My writing, I am prepared to think, may be a substitute for something I*

have been born without – a so-called normal relation to society. My books are my relation to society.

The more I read of the letters between Southall and his admirers, the more I begin to wonder about the reader-writer relationship and its peculiar non-physical, even quasi-metaphysical nature. Perhaps Bowen was right and this is the only kind of relationship that writers can successfully have, that which is mediated by books.

There are few other relationships in life outside the reader-writer connection that can be so intense and emotional without the people involved actually getting to know each other in the flesh. But perhaps the fact that the reader and writer do not know each other "in the real world" is precisely what makes it so special. If a reader wants to be in the presence of her favourite author, she doesn't need to call or email or try to find a space in her diary to meet at a café or in a bar – she simply opens up a book. And if a writer wants to speak to her readers, all she need do is sit down with her pen or her laptop. They meet only in a shared imaginary world: a strange yet intimate mental and emotional space, where both are always free to stay or to go.

I wonder whether this utter freedom, the idea of a relationship without worldly constraints, might be the cause of my deeply troubled romantic history. Because compared to the reader-writer relationship, every other kind of relationship, saddled as it is with responsibilities and schedules and shopping lists, seems so difficult and dull in comparison. The writer is to the reader what he or she wishes him to be: a hero, a friend, a confidante, a lover, or a character from one of the writer's books.

"They turn to me as if I were a brother a little older," says Southall, "far enough ahead to have gained a little wisdom, but close enough to touch, not knowing me as I am, a grandfather many years and ten thousand miles removed. They picture me as Josh or Michael or Max or Matt – or Frances or Jan or Abigail. Are they victims of a delusion? Or am I?"

* * *

Reading through the hundreds of letters to Southall has given me the desire to get in touch with some of the young correspondents that are now adults. Did they have a similar experience to mine? Given that in most cases at least fifty years had elapsed since the then-child put pen to paper, getting in touch will involve some intense detective work, much of it undertaken, with the skills of a private investigator, by my NLA colleague.

First on my list is Sue Harrington, a young girl from a convent school in Perth who wrote to Southall in the early 1970s. Of all the letters I have perused, hers are the most intimate:

①

Ref 16·4·73
Balloon
Sel

7 Calpin Cres,
Attadale.
W.A 6156
Perth 10·4·73.

Dear Ivan,

My name is Sue Harrington and I have just turned 12 and I go to Santa Maria College. I'm writing to tell you how I feel about you and your books, no, its going to be bad so don't worry. I have read these books of yours and enjoyed them. Bread & Honey, Hills end. To the wild sky I was fortunate to have read Bread & Honey first and it really shook me up, then I became aware of your kind of flabogasting writing now you are my favourite autor.

②.

you are very special to me in lots of ways. Just like my boyfriend. I'm just finishing my homework and doing a book report on TO THE WILD SKY. Please keep writing more mo books like Bread & Honey cause I love them. My teacher at school said some old people didn't approve of your kind of writing But I think its rubbish and so does she so keep writing. As I said before you're very special you've put my thinking a long way ahead. I know to you're very busy but I would like to sought of have you for a great pen friend if you can rasg man-age it. If you could when you write back send me any book of yours, your favourite to me with this written on it

" Dear Sue

Ivan Southall " if you like. P.T.O.

Not withstanding the author's overwhelming commitments – which by then included supporting a wife and four children, the youngest with Down syndrome – Southall embarked on a pen friendship, enclosing, at Sue's request, an autographed book.

Sue writes back:

> *Thanks a lot for the book. I was really thrilled … I suppose you have been battling with mail but I felt I needed to talk to someone as I'm not really happy right now. Tell you why later. I'm in a large family of 10. 5 girls and 3 boys and I find a big gap in relationships, especially with parents. They can't seem to see me. My mother died long ago and I now have another who doesn't seem to understand me. I'm always getting picked on "do this, do that". But if the same thing is wrong with the others they don't get in trouble. I can't tell them anything, I must work it out on my own … That's why I say I think you would be a good dad, you would understand, I think. Can you suggest any way I can talk over problems with my parents as most kids can? I find I won't be able to go on on my own forever, as I'm now 12.*

Southall replies:

Dear Sue,

I was touched by your letter and very honoured that you should write to me as a friend. I really can't tell you how to approach your parents because I don't know them. I don't know their situation, or their problems, or their moods, but I do tell kids sometimes (face to face as well as in books) that parents have real problems too. Living is great fun, it's exciting, it's happy – it's all sorts of good things, but nothing can be good unless we have something to measure. That is why we have dreary times, dull times and sad times. We have got to have it both ways, we have got to accept it both ways, because without the one we cannot have the other.

In Southall, Sue finds someone who truly listens. She writes long, heartfelt letters, sometimes enclosing her own experiments in creative writing:

7 Calpin Cres,
Attadale. Perth,
WA. 6156.

Dear Ivan,

Hi. Thanks for your very nice letter it means a lot to me. Enclosed is my poem, if it is fitting to class it as poetry. But never the less it was written for you, and so i guess now you can read it, laugh at it or think about it or burn it as i intended doing.

I've left it the way it was originally so it may be very bad english etc (i'm hopeless at english) and may have lots of mistakes but now it's yours. in all its confusion of whether to be happy or sad about your visit + your going back home.

I find it quite amusing recalling the state of mind i wrote it in, i was so mixed up.

I know i'm a really bad letter writer, & i apologize for this but i guess it's the only way to communicate with my (best) friend.

Since i've known you i've tried to reveal who i really am and i hope my poem may help you to know me better. I've shared things with you that i'd never tell anyone else & i hope to share more of myself with you in the future.S.K I may not be very good at explaining myself at times and sharing with you, but i hope you know i certainly try.

Not much happening over here, but hope you're fine and would you say hi to your family for me (if you have time (ha)) Thanks abt for everything.

your true friend,
Sue.

When I finally track down Sue Harrington she is as thrilled to hear from me as I am to have found her. "My relationship with Ivan was one of the most important of my life," she tells me.

The following week the staff of the National Library install me in a conference room with a large screen for a Skype interview with Sue. "That letter writing with Ivan gave me a sense of freedom to say whatever I was thinking," she says, "and it was always surprising that he would respond, and that was a really unique thing, because I had never been able to express worries or concerns or anything face to face with anybody with that degree of honesty, particularly with adults.

"My life at that time was caught up with the day-to-day practicalities and rules. If Dad spoke to me at all, it was about minding my manners or saying my prayers. My father was very distant, very strict. He was an engineer so he was mathematical and methodical. And because we were so many kids, I never had an individual relationship with my father. I was just one of many. We never had a personal conversation about what I might be feeling."

Is this because the role of fathering back in the 1960s was simply to provide financially for the family? Did dads ever have personal conversations with their children then? Certainly my father never did, despite being at the forefront of the allegedly more open sixties movement. I don't remember my father ever sharing an intimacy or a childhood memory. He never once reminisced about his three younger sisters, or the sheep station he grew up on in remote Western Australia or his father's deep sorrow when his only son ran away to London to study, forcing the sale of the farm my grandfather had spent his entire life building.

It was only from my aunt Rachel, my father's closest sister, that I learnt about the spider orchids my father loved to pick and the suitcase of birds' eggs he kept under his bed. It was only after his death I heard the story of how he received a Hale school uniform for his twelfth birthday, and then spent the next six years as an unhappy boarder in Perth, hundreds of miles from his family in Geraldton.

As I grew older, my father and I began going on regular bushwalks and this opened the way for more conversation. However, it was still restricted to philosophy and politics – his favourite topics – carefully remaining abstract enough to steer clear of feelings. I never learnt how my parents met, what their wedding was like, why they had separated and got back together again and separated yet again. And I knew it wasn't polite to ask.

Southall was also reticent with his children, always finding it easier to express himself emotionally on paper than in person. His daughter, Elizabeth, commented that her father "could write emotion but couldn't handle it". Perhaps this is why he achieved an intimacy with Susan Harrington that he couldn't with his own children.

Ivan Southall's generous friendship with Sue as an adolescent in Western Australia in the early 1970s made such an impact on her life that when she turned thirty-five, she decided to seek him out to express her gratitude: "It was one of those mid-life crisis kind of things and I was thinking about all the people who had got me where I was at, about who was important and who I had just let disappear. There were a few people I wanted to contact and thank; Ivan Southall was one of them."

By this time, Southall was living in Healesville, Victoria, with his second wife, Susan. "I remember sitting in their lounge room and thanking him for helping me through that period," said Sue. "He asked me about my family and work. He showed me his desk and his study, where he wrote. We didn't really talk about anything personal or in depth. And then he showed me his fuchsias." Southall had always been a gardener and towards the end of his life he specialised in fuchsias, collecting hundreds and cultivating new varieties that he registered with the American Fuchsia Society.

Sue admits that the real-life meeting with Southall was "a little bit of an anti-climax": "I came to understand it as a reiteration of the fact that sometimes people are more honest in their writing. Or at least you get to know them better through their writing than you do when you're face to face. The books allow more honesty and openness. Perhaps when you read something a person has written you see more into their true nature."

From my own experience, I was aware that when meeting a literary idol, there is often a risk of disappointment. As a very young aspiring writer I had travelled to England to meet my favourite living writer, with whom I had corresponded for a number of years. But I was too young and pretty at the time for The Great Man to take me seriously. The parts of me that received his attention were not the parts I wanted him to notice. Then again, I had arrived with no evidence of talent so there was no reason for him to take me seriously. During the time it took the famous writer to drive from the station to his country cottage, I was in such a state of anxiety that when we arrived I cast desperately around for some way to leave. I excused myself by saying I wanted to go for a walk in the English countryside I had spent my life reading about in 19th century novels. I walked for three hours, hoping I might re-find the train station and escape. By the time I returned to the house the lunch was spoiled and my literary idol was perplexed. Why had this whippersnapper travelled all the way from Australia only to disappear? These Antipodeans were profoundly strange. Our return trip to the train station swung between silence and over-excited prattle. I sat in a hot state of embarrassment all the way back to London. It was my first experience of confronting the difference between a writer and his books.

Are we writers true on the page but untrue in life? Or unreal on the page and real in life? I might suggest that the "true nature" that Sue refers to is actually a highly manufactured presentation that has been worked over incessantly, reshaped and edited for the reader's consumption. What ends up in a printed book is the best of a person; in fact, the whole idea of writing a book, with its book covers acting as firm boundaries, is to shield the reader from all the things that make writers notoriously impossible to live with in real life. Certainly, Southall's domestic life was no picnic. From all accounts, he and his wife Joy had a fraught marriage, made more difficult by perpetual financial problems and a disabled child, which eventually ended in a bitter divorce. My own case is even worse: two divorces and a broken ten-year relationship leaving a wound that is still wide open. But of course this is the place from which most of us write – from out of the wound.

I decide not to tell Sue about how wounded and flawed I believe all writers are and suggest instead that perhaps we are talking about two types of reality that correspond to two very distinct types of human relationship: the reality of the everyday world, of washing machines and workplaces and thorny marriages; and the reality of the imagined world, of fiction and friendship and long-distance letters, which is also necessarily a very private world.

The Irish novelist John McGahern describes the reader-writer relationship thus:

> In a way I think each of us inhabit a private world that others cannot see and it's that world with which we read. The only difference between the reader and the writer is that the writer has the instinct or the talent to dramatise that private world. And that private world actually doesn't come alive again until the reader brings it to life in their private world.

In *A Journey of Discovery* (1975), Southall's book about writing for children, he refers to the novel as a private experience that ideally "is an exchange of the truth in the strictest confidence between two people" (the reader and the writer), suggesting that such "naked truth" is much more difficult to achieve between two people in ordinary, everyday relationships.

I am beginning to believe that this is at the crux of my current crisis. As a child, I discovered the intense, transcendental nature of McGahern's magic, metaphysical, private world – a world that protected me from the reality of silently separating parents, of an overworked, long-suffering mother, of the awareness of a foreign war that had led to the conscription of school friends' older brothers and was occupying my obsessive anti-war activist father day and night. Ever since then, I have chosen this private world over the real world, constantly retreating into words and books. I have learnt that this kind of avoidance can attract a diagnosable label: it's called adjustment disorder, the DSM category for people who cannot adjust to reality.

* * *

I continue my quest to speak to as many Southall correspondents as I can find in an effort to find out what effect he had on them. I speak to Graham Betley and Janie de Souza in Melbourne, Christeen Scheopf in Port Augusta, Vernon Hyden in Cairns, Monica Eather in Albury, Ione Rummery in California, and Annette Weinhues in Germany.

The correspondents, all of them now at least in their mid-fifties, are always delighted to hear from me. All of them remember Southall, recall writing to him, and many of them still treasure his replies. All are heartened to think that the author bothered to keep their childish notes. Although these readers often don't recall the specific plots of Southall books, they all retain the deep impression of the reading experience and easily remember the titles that affected them most. Many have carried the hardbacks with them all their lives, through changes of home and even shifts in country. Despite the decades that have passed, the books remain a deeply felt memory that is stronger, for most, than any other book of that period. The word most often used to describe the experience of reading Southall is "intense", an adjective that could be equally applied to the author as an individual.

"The work's quite atomic," says Mark Mordue, 59, and still a devoted fan. "It's compressed and close, there's a real intimacy in it; there is always one person you're utterly locked in on. It's definitely a love relationship between you and the character. You enter it and become it, but I also think that it's therefore a love relationship between you and the writer." Southall would have agreed. "You reach those and please those who tune in on your wavelength," he writes. "It is a very personal matter. Rapport – no less and probably no more. If it is there, it is something like a love affair, and even children fall in love."

I am just one of many who fell in love with Ivan Southall. So perhaps this is the real nature of the reader-writing relationship – one of a long-distance, non-physical love affair. And if so, maybe it represents the ultimate, ethereal transcendent love, independent of the material world. A love that is purely spiritual, that both children and adults can experience. The only love, perhaps, that is truly perfect.

My return to Canberra, I realise, isn't really about looking for the origins of my writing life. I am looking for love. But like all my relationships with men, my love for Southall, although intense and fiery, is finite. I no longer admire his novels unreservedly. Perhaps part of the problem with Southall is the same problem I've had with all my boyfriends, husbands, and lovers. What attracts me – their inscrutable and ultimately unknowable maleness – is also, in the end, what repels me.

Among the devoted readers of Southall, I find a number of contemporary writers. Memoirist Ailsa Piper tells me that, "*Ash Road* and *To the Wild Sky* made me feel that my own story was something that had a place in the world of books. That those cloth-bound treasures were not only about people 'up there' on the other side of the world, but that they could also be opened to reveal me and my friends." Novelist James Roy writes in a collection called *The Book that Made Me,* "Most young readers want a story that makes them feel something they recognise, something that makes them feel better about being who they are, and about being the way they are. For me, *Josh* was that book."

For children's author Jenny Pausacker, Ivan Southall is "the Patrick White of children's fiction". When she heard him give a lecture in 1974, it was a turning point in her life and her career. "I still go like melted butter at the thought of it," she says. "He was fantastic. I saw him early on in my writing for children and it gave me a sense of vocation and destiny. He was so inspiring."

Journalist, editor, and non-fiction writer Mark Mordue feels so indebted to Southall that in 2003 he penned "The Secret Life of Us", an homage for *Australian Author*:

> Southall established a world for me that was adventurous, harshly sensuous, distressingly solitary and distinctly Australia. In books such as *Ash Road, To the Wild Sky* and *Finn's Folly* he helped me fall in love with reading; he also put me on the path to becoming a writer.

"I wrote that piece," says Mordue, "to say thank-you to Southall. I believe he was *the* children's writer of the last century. To me personally he was as important as C.S. Lewis. At minimum he wrote half a dozen classics for Australian children but where is the recognition? Where is his plaque? Where is the prize in his honour? He had a decade of being the best children's writer in the country, recognised the world over, and a few decades later he is utterly forgotten. It's a bit of a lesson for people who are this month's flavour."

Southall responded to Mordue's essay with a letter:

> *Personally, "The Secret Life of Us" has put heart into me, warmed me: thank you. For so long I've lived the life of a target; then as an object to be ignored, belittled or written off as probably dead.*

"When I read that letter, which had so much feeling in it, I thought, what a cruel country we are," says Mordue. "We undervalue people here. The cultural cringe is as alive as it ever was. Southall spoke to an entire generation of children and probably a lot of writers were born through him but for some reason in Australia we feel compelled to forget the past and be eternally caught up in an infantile present."

Mark's comment immediately reminds me of the final line from *Bread and Honey.* When Michael's grandmother is preparing to place a wreath on the ANZAC memorial, he asks, "Is this because people remember, Grandma, or pretend that they don't forget?"

Southall referred to the height of his literary fame as his "crest of clarity", a wave that had begun with *Hills End* and peaked with his Carnegie Medal for *Josh* (1971). In the decades that followed, the crest took a dive, and by the 1990s he felt all but forgotten. There were new players on the YA literary scene and literature, like anything else, is vulnerable to fashion. Southall's style of adventure story no longer appealed.

By the time of his death in 2008, the Ivan Southall phenomenon that had swept Australia in the 1960s and 1970s, influencing tens of thousands of young readers, both here and overseas, with translations into over twenty languages, had been all but erased from our cultural memory.

"We all have our moments," says Drew, who grew up to be an accomplished visual artist and sculptor. "I had mine in

1979." But when his father's moment passed, says Drew, the author couldn't cope: "I observed him in his last few years, as one creative artist observing another. I've seen it in some artist friends as they got older. They ended up painting shit. They were kidding themselves that they were being really creative but it's just awful. I don't think Dad was any different to that."

Perhaps this is the real cause of my dilemma: I have had my moment and I am having difficulty admitting it. "One's prime is elusive," says Miss Jean Brodie to her students. "You little girls, when you grow up, must be on the alert to recognise your prime at whatever time of your life it may occur. You must then live it to the full. Attend to me, girls. One's prime is the moment one was born for." For years I have been waiting for my prime, but perhaps my crisis of faith requires nothing more or less than facing up to the simple fact that I am past my prime, or even worse, never reached it.

Southall once wrote that "the only choice the writer has is to face life as his own experience has revealed it." And yet, the fact that his crest had fallen and flattened out was not something that Southall wanted to face up to. The title of his unpublished autobiography, *Delights Gained from Being Obsolete*, leaves no doubt as to how he felt about finding himself, after all that attention, suddenly and permanently passé.

* * *

After my father died, we cleared out his office at the university where he had worked for the last thirty-seven years. In his filing cabinet, I found an old khaki folder labelled "Gabrielle", bulging with drawings and paintings from my preschool days. One drawing, repeated over and over, was a portrait of a lady, smiling and slightly wobbly, wearing a long dress, overlaid with an apron. On the apron was a design of a cottage with a smoking chimney: a gentle, domestic picture of what I envisioned for my future – a happy, grown-up mother and wife in a pretty dress and pinafore. Perhaps if not for Southall, I would have become a housewife devoted to her family, free of writerly yearnings.

When you make the decision to become a writer at the age of nine, much of the ordinary, everyday schoolwork becomes irrelevant. By the time I was in high school, I had lost interest altogether. Then one afternoon, at the age of fifteen, completely unexpectedly, the turning point arrived. I was in my Domestic Science class; in those days, it was an all-girls subject for which it was compulsory to wear a white apron. That particular day, I had forgotten my apron, possibly deliberately. My punishment was to be banished to the adjoining equipment room to scrub saucepans that were already clean. Infuriated, I picked up my bag and strode out of the class and then out of the school grounds and walked home.

My father, who was mostly absent from home and from my life, suddenly became very concerned that I had decided to leave school without having completed my school certificate.

After much negotiation, it was arranged that I would enrol in another local school, Sylvania High, just long enough to complete the Year 10 exams. I acquiesced because there was only six weeks of term left and afterwards, I told myself, it would all be over. I could at last leave the classroom and *become a writer.* Whereas Southall's enforced withdrawal from school at fourteen was a deprivation that he never quite got over, I found the prospect of abandoning my formal education at fifteen positively liberating.

* * *

When he was very young, Ivan showed a story to his father, hoping it would win him praise. The story was so good that Frank Southall didn't believe his son could have written it and smacked him for telling lies. Decades later, Ivan still remembered the hurt it caused when he recounted the story to his grown-up daughter Elizabeth.

In 2010, while Southall was dying of cancer, Elizabeth read to him aloud. By then he was also suffering from dementia. One afternoon, Elizabeth read her father *Fly West* (1974), one of his own novels. When she got to the end, he looked at her and with feeling announced: "That author can really write."

* * *

After three months in Canberra I pack up my numerous folders containing interview transcripts, copies of children's letters and a spreadsheet of Southall correspondents. It is time to return to Sydney and attempt to put my pen to paper and try to make sense of what I have found. All this research had been fascinating and fun but I couldn't delay the hard part – the writing – any longer.

For months I wrestle with my material. Occasionally I feel myself warming to Southall once more but then I go cold again. I know in my bones that it is wrong to write a biography about a person you do not love so each word feels like a wrench and a betrayal. I draft and re-draft but the book refuses emerge. I can't believe that I have spent so much of my life hunched over a desk and yet still do not know how to write. Each new project is like starting out all over again, as though I have learnt nothing at all.

Amidst this seemingly futile struggle to deliver a book I have promised to the National Library, among various others, I get a message from Drew Southall saying that he is coming to Sydney. I suggest we meet for lunch in Centennial Park, where I can interview him in person.

At seventy, Drew is craggy with shoulder-length grey hair but the remains of his good looks, inherited from his father, are still evident. I shake his hand and we move to a table on the veranda of the Centennial Homestead restaurant. Tall and leggy, Drew folds himself into the chair and then looks at me intently from across the table. I apologise for being late and refrain from offering him a compensatory drink. I have learnt from his autobiography that Drew is now abstinent.

Ivan's son has bright blue eyes, intense and searching, just like his father's. I feel – I know – I have to be very careful. I want to avoid revealing my misgivings about Southall or seeming too critical, and yet I realise how transparent I am; my feelings show, especially while in the glare of such an incisive, intelligent gaze.

The truth is that my feelings about my childhood literary hero, at this point, are almost overwhelmingly negative. As an adult with decades of reading behind me and possibly an over-developed critical faculty, I now find Southall's writing frustrating in style and substance. He is preoccupied with boys and masculinity, his protagonists are perpetually misunderstood, the adults relentlessly bullying and ignorant, and his tone whiney. Worst of all, there is not even a modicum of humour. Then again, much of my own work might also be accused of humourlessness so how can I hold this against him?

I order a salad and Drew decides on fish and chips.

"You have a drink if you like," he encourages.

So I ask for a Grenache, even though I never drink at lunch time. It is only then I realise how nervous I am.

I begin by talking to Drew about his own book, *But: A Journey of Addiction* (1997). Until forty, he was a daily drinker. Then a friend introduced him to a twelve-step program.

While in London in the 1980s, Drew briefly attended ACOA meetings, for Adult Children of Alcoholics.

"I am the adult child of an addict," says Drew. "My father was basically a workaholic. He had to be. I have no doubt about that. You do not do what he achieved by being a so-called normal, well-adjusted person. I don't believe it's possible. I don't think that Dad could have done what he did without being obsessive-compulsive and that's another way of describing an addict."

Throughout the interview, Drew is startlingly candid, answering all my questions without reservation. He wants to be faithful to reality, another feature often attributed to his father who refused to allow any prettying-up of the world in his stories for children.

After lunch, Drew pulls out his phone and shows me a recently completed drawing titled "Self-Portrait 181". It is mercilessly honest, every crease of his well-worn face meticulously drawn. There is something powerfully impressive about his comfort with his body, the opposite of Southall, who had always been ill at ease in his own skin.

"And so how would you describe your relationship with Ivan?" I ask.

Drew answers without hesitation. "I hated my father. As far back as I can remember, I hated him."

It was only when Drew became a professional artist that there was some understanding and mutual respect between the two men, but never any intimacy. I wonder if, towards the end, perhaps they became closer.

"I saw him three days before he died," he says.

"And did you feel reconciled?"

"No."

For a moment we fall into silence.

"And the funeral?"

"I didn't go."

Again, there is a pause.

"Three reasons why I didn't go. I don't like funerals. I find them utterly insincere and I knew this was going to be fucking insincere. My mother was going to be there, carrying on, and I was really angry about that at the time. I mean, Susan didn't count; it was all about Mum and Dad. And my two daughters were going to be there, and my sister Robbie, and I wasn't talking to any of them."

I am stunned. Not by the fact that he didn't attend Ivan's funeral or wasn't speaking to his mother or his sister or his daughters. But by his frankness, his honesty, and his complete acceptance of his own feelings. I suddenly realise that I have never met anyone even remotely like him.

But then again, maybe I have.

Drew goes on to reminisce about his teenage years growing up on Blackwood Farm in rural Victoria. "I used to go past Plumber and Son in Monbulk and think, *why the hell does the son have to be a plumber, too?* But why am I an artist? Because

I grew up with a writer. Regardless of whether I liked him or not, or hated him …"

I interrupt: "You turned into him."

"Yes," said Drew. "Absolutely."

After lunch, I walk dreamily through the park, feeling as though I have discovered an old friend from childhood. There is something about Drew that feels instantly familiar – like the time I re-met my first cousin after forty years and we so easily reignited our relationship, unmarred by the adult conflicts, corruptions and disappointments that would have inevitably arisen if we had grown up together.

Southall's son and I had both been bequeathed something by his father: Drew the compulsion to draw and I the inspiration to write. The same man who set Drew's life on a particular path also set mine – a path that at times feels like a gift and at other times a curse. We are therefore, in some mysterious way, deeply related.

I sit waiting for my bus for a long time, feeling inexplicably happy and grateful, certain that I have unexpectedly discovered a kindred spirit.

The same feeling I'd had when I was nine years old.

Bibliography

Archive

All written correspondence between Ivan Southall and his readers was accessed from the Papers of Ivan Southall, (MS5379) National Library of Australia, Canberra. The letters reproduced are from Boxes 6 and 7 of that collection. Some of the written correspondence presented in this essay have had minor alterations made to punctuation and spelling for ease of reading. All efforts have been made to contact the original correspondents. Some surnames have been redacted to ensure privacy.

Interviews conducted by the author

Allbrook, Martin. 31 March 2017.

Barber (née Southall), Elizabeth. 21 August 2017.

Mordue, Mark. 5 August 2017.

Marsden, John. 21 April 2017.

Murray, Kirsty. 13 October 2017.

Pausacker, Jenny. 5 May 2017.

Piper, Ailsa. 24 October 2017.

Southall, Andrew. 6 October 2017.

Southall, Susan. 20 May 2017.

Southall, Joy. 21 August 2017.

Works by Ivan Southall

Meet Simon Black, Angus & Robertson, Sydney, 1950.

They Shall Not Pass Unseen, Angus & Robertson, Sydney, 1956.

Simon Black and the Space Men, Angus & Robertson, Sydney, 1958.

Hills End, Angus & Robertson, Sydney and London, 1962.

Ash Road, Angus & Robertson, Sydney and London, 1965.

To the Wild Sky, Angus & Robertson, Sydney and London, 1967.

Let the Balloon Go, Angus & Robertson, Sydney and London, 1968.

Finn's Folly, Angus & Robertson, Sydney and London, 1969.

Bread and Honey, Angus & Robertson, Sydney and London, 1970.

Josh, Angus & Robertson, Sydney and London, 1971.

Fly West, Angus & Robertson, Sydney and London, 1974.

A Journey of Discovery: On writing for children, Macmillan, New York, 1976.

What About Tomorrow?, Angus & Robertson, Sydney and London, 1977.

A City Out of Sight, Angus & Robertson, Sydney, 1984.

Hills End, Text Publishing, Melbourne, 2013.

Books

Amis, Martin. *The Information*, Harper Collins, London, 1995.

Bowen, Elizabeth; Greene, Graham & Pritchett, V.S. *Why Do I Write?*, P. Marshall, London, 1948.

Muriel, Spark. *The Prime of Miss Jean Brodie*, Macmillan, London, 1961.

Nieuwenhuizen, Agnes. *The Written World: Youth and Literature*, D.W. Thorpe, Port Melbourne, 1994.

Roy, James. 'James Remembering', *The Book that Made Me*, Walker Books, Sydney, 2016.

Southall, Drew. *But: A Journey into Addiction*, Hudson Publishing, Kew, 1997.

Steggall, Stephanie. *The Loved and the Lost: The Life of Ivan Southall,* Lothian Books Melbourne, 2006.

Other works

Collins, Pat [Dir.]. *John McGahern: A Private World*, Harvest Films, 2005.

De Berg, Hazel & Clune, Frank. *Papers of Hazel de Berg,* National Library of Australia, 2005.

Kafka, Franz. 'Letter to Oskar Pollack', *Letters to Family, Friends, and Editors*, Schocken Books, 1977 [1904].

McGorry, Paddy. 'Growing Up Male: Ivan Southall's View', *Refractory Girl*, Spring 1973.

McVitty, Walter. 'Wounding and Regeneration', *Innocence & Experience: Essays on Contemporary Australian Children's Writers*, Nelson, Melbourne, 1981.

Mordue, Mark. 'The Secret Life of Us', *Australian Author*, Vol. 35, No. 1, Apr. 2003, pp. 8–16.

Parks, Tim. 'Does Literature Help Us Live?', *New York Review of Books*, 3 Aug. 2018.

Pausacker, Jenny. 'Not Under Glass: The Novels of Ivan Southall.' *Meanjin*, Vol. 51, No. 3, 1992.

Southall, Andrew. Unpublished poem, 2017.

Southall, Ivan. 'Delights Gained from Being Obsolete', unpublished manuscript.

Ivan Southall Papers, National Library of Australia: http://nla.gov.au/nla.ms-ms5379, 1914–2009.

Wighton, Rosemary. 'Novels for Children', *Australian Book Review*, Vol. 10, 1972.

www.ingramcontent.com/pod-product-compliance
Ingram Content Group Australia Pty Ltd
76 Discovery Rd, Dandenong South VIC 3175, AU
AUHW020910070726
429584AU00004B/51